D1522029

Living while BLACK

MY EXPERIENCE *with* "EVERYDAY RACISM"

BEVERLY HARRIS-SCHENZ

Beverly Harris-Schenz
3323 Shady Avenue Extension
Pittsburgh, PA 15217

"Routine Traffic Stop in June 2017" first appeared in *Voices in the Attic,* vol xxvi, 2020, pp. 67-69. It is reprinted here with permission of Carlow University Press.

Ordering Information, for details contact: bharrisschenz@gmail.com

Print ISBN: 979-8-35091-484-9
eBook ISBN: 979-8-35091-485-6

Printed in the United States of America on SFI Certified paper

First Edition

In memory of my father, Samuel, in honor of my mother, Mary, and in loving appreciation of my husband, Michael

Table Contents

INTRODUCTION

At this point in my life, I am reflecting on the experiences and people that have shaped me and helped me successfully navigate the world that I inhabited as an African American woman. I attended premier universities for both my undergraduate and graduate education. I have been privileged and grateful to have had a 38-year career at both professorial and administrative levels at three major universities. In my field of German Studies, it was (and is) extremely rare to see a German professor with my skin tone. In addition, my personal life has also been somewhat atypical because I have shared it with my husband of 47 years, who is a German National and Caucasian.

As a person of color in this country, I have had to learn to function and thrive according to the norms and expectations established and upheld by people whose skin color I do not share. Out of necessity, I have developed a strong sense of self and a tough exterior to endure perennial examples of "everyday racism." Often subtle but pervasive, the bias is constant. This reality for most Black Americans is independent of education, socioeconomic or professional status, place of residence, depth of intellect, or content of character. When I venture out into the world, I am seen first and foremost as the inhabitant of my skin color, which then determines how I am perceived and treated.

However, this cacophony of off-hand comments, "unintentional" oversights and slights, dismissive comments, and the inability to recognize or accept our intelligence or authority are frequently invisible to our White counterparts. Why? Because they have never had these experiences. They are oblivious to the tedious and often onerous burden of "living while Black." A White person will often assume that either such situations do not exist or are hopelessly exaggerated by those who do experience them. These daily microaggressions can, over time, engender self-doubt, frustration, anger, stress, and sometimes significant health problems for those who are seen as "less than." My life has not been the exception. For this reason, it is to these situations in my own experience, these microaggressions, these moments of "living while Black," that I dedicate the autobiographical vignettes in this volume.

Considering recent public examples of blatant racism, violence, and disrespect toward African Americans, there is a tendency to focus understandably on the myriad examples of systemic or institutional racism and their dire consequences. However, due to the prevalence and frequent disavowal of the numerous micro-inequities that Black people confront daily, I feel strongly that we must identify, face, and address these situations, if we ever wish to eradicate them and their negative impact. If we want to create a society that lives up to its creed that "all people are created equal" then we must guarantee that all people are also treated equally in their daily interactions. However, first it is necessary to educate those who do not see the problem.

In a conversation with Rabbi Ethan Linden, he once described with candor a situation in which he saw, for the first time, the limitations of his lived experience. He had invited a Black man who had recently been released from prison to be a guest at his Passover seder. The man shared his story of having served more than 20 years for a crime he did not commit. Rabbi Linden remembered:

> And in that moment, I realized I did not understand freedom, not really, and I did not know this man, or his life. And further, it seemed to me then, and it seems to me now, that to be a responsible citizen of this multitudinous country, I would need to do a much better job imagining the lives of those who are not me, and do not have my life.

Linden's statement supports the adage that to truly understand another person's issues and concerns, we "must walk a mile in someone else's shoes." But realistically, it is impossible to do that, isn't it? In our country, where the lives of Black and White Americans are often lived in de facto apartheid from each other, it is understandable that White people are often ignorant of the day-to-day reality of the lived experiences of their Black fellow citizens. Since a White person cannot become Black for a day or a few hours to get a better understanding of what that life is really like, how then could even a well-intentioned White person develop empathy or understanding for others whose lives are so different?

Webster defines empathy as "identifying with and understanding another's situation, feelings, and motives." In African cultures, however, the definition of being human is expressed in the concept of "ubuntu," which recognizes that "my humanity is bound up in yours, for we can only be human together."[1] Archbishop Desmond Tutu goes even further, when he states emphatically,

> I would not know how to be a human being at all except I learned this from other human beings. We are made for a delicate network of relationships, of interdependence. We are meant to complement each other.[2]

If our goal is to complement each other then certainly understanding each other is an essential first step. However, in today's America, it is increasingly difficult to see our commonalities. Tribalism is writ large, and our society is increasingly divided between insiders and outsiders, us and them, red and blue, and the fault lines that divide us seem much wider and deeper than they used to be. In a commencement address

1   Naomi Tutu, ed, The Words of Desmond Tutu (New York: Newmarket Press, 1989), p. 71
2   Tutu, p. 73

in 2006, then Senator Barack Obama bemoaned the "empathy deficit," which he felt characterized our country. Since then, and perhaps ironically in no small part as a backlash to Obama's two terms in the White House, things have only grown worse. The existing healthcare disparities along racial lines made more glaring by the pandemic, the desperate economic dislocation of so many, as well as the spotlight that has been placed on systemic racism highlighted by continued police violence against Black people, illustrate clearly that we are not "all in this together." Conversations between Americans of different racial and ethnic groups, political beliefs, educational experience, genders, sexual orientations, and incomes were always challenging, but even more so now.

In his book *War for Kindness: Building Empathy in a Fractured World*, Stanford professor Jamil Zaki explores the concept of empathy and identifies three ways that people respond to each other:

1. Identifying what others feels (cognitive empathy)
2. Sharing emotion (emotional empathy)
3. Wishing to improve other's experiences (empathic concern)[3]

In considering the three forms of empathetic response, Zaki concludes that cognitive empathy is the most useful way

3   Zaki, p. 81.

to learn about another's experiences. Through the process of "mentalizing," he writes, "We develop a fine-grained picture of not just what someone else feels, but why they feel it. . ."[4] Contrary to many researchers before him, Zaki asserts that empathy is not an immutable trait, but rather a skill that can be developed with practice. The question then becomes, how can we practice empathy for those with whom we do not come in direct contact or whose experiences are distinct from our own?

Psychologist Raymond Mar provides an answer to this question. He examined the role of reading fiction in developing empathy and determined that "novels and stories give people a chance to experience countless lives."[5] By reading the stories and experiences of others, fictional or not, readers can put themselves in their place and transport themselves to a different reality. Zaki affirms our ability to do this when he states that "Empathy is the mental superpower that overcomes this distance. Through it we voyage to others' worlds and make guesses about how it feels to be them."[6]

* * *

In the collection of stories that follow, I am inviting you to join me on a voyage of exploration, one that will give readers the

---

4   Zaki, p. 181.
5   Zaki, p. 81
6   Zaki, p. 4.

opportunity to step into shoes that may feel very different from their own. Regardless of who you are, everyone has, at some time, for some reason, felt excluded and an outsider. You may well have experienced differential or unequal treatment from someone who sized you up based not on your personhood but because of your race or ethnicity, gender or sexual orientation, age, educational level, economic status, or intellectual or physical challenge. To paraphrase Isabel Wilkerson[7], someone has placed us in a box not of our own making or design. In my case, the "box" is clearly labeled Black and female.

Each vignette in this collection describes a discrete personal experience of racial or gender bias. Black readers may not have shared these exact situations but will likely nod in agreement as they read and recall similar encounters. They can supplement these episodes with experiences and feelings of their own. White readers, on the other hand, may be totally surprised and unaware that such incidents occur, or consider them to be exaggerated, unique, coincidental, and even unrelated altogether to racial bias or implicit racism. They can think about the events and consider what feelings are elicited in those involved, as well as what actions and beliefs may have precipitated them. Since empathy is a skill, the different vignettes

7   Isabel Wilkerson, *Caste: The Origins of our Discontents* (New York: Random House, 2020).

provide readers opportunities to practice "mentalizing" and thus strengthening their empathic response.

Each vignette is accompanied by discussion questions intended to expand recognition, understanding, and empathy. It is my hope that learning about and discussing my travails, drawn from several decades of life and work, will offer others a "contact-lite" means of "understanding and walking in another's shoes." Such conversations will invariably be challenging and thought-provoking. But they are also essential if we want to take steps to breach the divisions that currently separate us and move toward a society that truly values each of its citizens.

MR. HARRIS

My father grew up in North Carolina. When my grandfather died in 1927, he left school in the sixth grade to help support his mother and seven sisters. During the Great Depression, he forged a strong work ethic and set high standards for himself. How often did I hear him say, "If you are going to do something, do it well, or not at all?" Regardless of the task, he expected excellence. Whether it was ironing shirts, polishing shoes, washing and waxing a car, or cleaning jewelry, there was no excuse for a shoddy job.

Coming of age in the South at a time when all Black men were "boys," my father insisted that other people treat him respectfully. As a child, I always wondered why my father introduced himself using only his last name. When meeting someone new, he would extend his hand, look the person in the eye, and say "Harris is my name. Pleased to meet you." It was only many years later that he told me that this self-designation ensured that no one knew or could use his first name. People who addressed him might not say mister, but they could not say "Samuel" or "Sam."

I never heard anyone call my father by his first name. In our extended family, respect for elders was a given and every child had to use a "handle" when addressing an adult. Non-family members were referred to as mister or miss plus first or last name. Adult relatives were called aunt, uncle, cousin, and close family friends were always aunt or uncle. Since my father was the second brother in his family, he was called "Little Brother," while his elder male sibling was "Brother." Since children were expected to show respect for elders, my cousins grew up calling my father, "Uncle Little Brother."

Within our family boundaries, this linguistic redundancy was expected, but in the world beyond, it appeared rather strange. When my father was sent a telegram by a niece, informing him of my grandmother's impending death, he was obliged to take it to the Chrysler Personnel Office to obtain bereavement leave. However, he was furious that the telegram was addressed to "Uncle Little Brother," and that he had to share this internal family anomaly with the external White world. Outside of the family, my father's friends and coworkers called him either Mr. Harris or Harris, and that extended to his in-laws, who also called him Harris. But, probably the most interesting example of this respectful formality is that my husband called his father-in-law "Mr. Harris" from the day they met until the day my father died more than 22 years later. That sounds odd, but it is easy to explain.

When the two men met, there were misgivings and reservations on both sides. My father, who was born in racially segregated North Carolina and had fought in WWII against the German enemy, was meeting his future son-in-law, who was White and German. My husband had reservations of his own: his future father-in-law, who had little formal education, spoke English with a Southern accent that he as a non-native English speaker found difficult to understand. Therefore, their initial interactions were cautious and tentative.

Gradually, they got better acquainted, found common subjects to talk about, and made adjustments for their unique personalities. But one thing never changed: my husband continued to call my father Mr. Harris.

As their relationship became more comfortable and relaxed, this nomenclature, though still linguistically formal, lost some of its emotional distance and stiffness. They laughed and talked easily, but my father never suggested that his son-in-law drop the "Mr." that preceded Harris or call him anything else. It was clear: he was, and would remain, Mr. Harris.

DISCUSSION QUESTIONS:

1. What do you think of Mr. Harris's strategy to demand respect from others? Do you think it was successful? Why or why not?

2. What is your reaction to the relationship between father and son-in-law?

3. If you had been this son-in-law, would you have done anything to address the issue of naming? Why or why not?

BUYING SHOES

Every fall, my father and I would meet at Crowley's, a large upscale department store in downtown Detroit, to purchase new school shoes. My father would be dressed in his crisply pressed Chrysler's uniform, and I would be wearing the plaid pleated skirt, knee socks and sweater-set that was the rage for high school girls in the early sixties. We went to Ladies Shoes on the sixth floor. Since shopping together happened only in the fall and at Easter, I was excited. After much back and forth, I selected two pairs: maroon Bass loafers and black and white saddle shoes.

The salesperson came over. "May I help you?"

"Yes, I would like to see these two pairs in a size 9 medium, please."

The salesman disappeared to find my size, while my father and I chatted about what had happened at school that day. Surprisingly, he was quite patient and enjoyed these shopping trips with his only child. The salesman returned, bringing my shoes. I tried them on, strolling around proudly, to see if they fit, and asking my father's opinion. He liked them and so did I.

"I will take both pairs," I told the salesman.

Returning shortly, he said, "The total will be $87." My father stood up, took out his money clip, peeled off a $100 bill, and handed it to the salesman. In those days, few Black people had credit cards.

The salesman took the bill, but when he glanced down, he hesitated.

"Do you have anything smaller?" he inquired.

"No," my father responded. "Is that a problem?"

"Oh, no, no. That will be fine," he said and turned away quickly.

Daddy and I continued to talk and waited for the salesman to return with my purchases and the change. However, five, ten, and then fifteen minutes passed, but still no salesman. My father was losing his patience.

"Where is he? Why isn't he coming? What is taking so long?" my father asked in quick succession.

I went to the counter, looked past it into the stock room, and saw the salesman speaking on the phone, in hushed tones. When he saw me, he paused.

"I am so sorry; I will be right out."

I left, but not before I heard him ask, "So, you think the bill is okay?"

I rushed back to my father. "Daddy, the salesman thinks the bill is counterfeit."

"And he doesn't have the courtesy to come back and say anything to me. I am just supposed to wait. Beverly, go and get my money."

Just as I got up, the salesman returned with the packages, and was about to speak, when my father said, "Please return my money."

"Sir, there is no problem, I—"

But my father interrupted him. "Yes, there is. This is not the only store in Detroit." He held out his hand, looked directly at him, and stood up. The $100 bill was returned.

The salesman started to speak, but my father continued, "I don't pay and beg. Come on, Beverly."

I stood up and followed my father in silence. As we took the down escalator, I was disappointed about not getting those shoes. However, I carried away a more important lesson. Everyone is due respect and courtesy, even a Black man in a Chrysler uniform.

DISCUSSION QUESTIONS:

1. How do you explain the behavior/motivation of the sales-person? Should he have done anything differently? If so, what?

2. Why were the police called in the George Floyd case? How is that more recent event related to this situation from 60 years prior?

3. How do you think Mr. Harris felt? How would you have felt in this situation?

4. Are you surprised by Mr. Harris's decision to leave? Why or why not?

5. How do you think his daughter felt about that decision?

MISS MARY AND HIGH SCHOOL ENGLISH

Unlike my father, my mother grew up in the North, in Hillsboro, a small town in Southern Illinois. She attended integrated schools there, and she and her twin sister were the sole Black students in the 1942 graduation class. She taught me self-reliance, confidence, and tenacity. In her worldview, nothing was impossible, but you had to work tirelessly, and excuses were not tolerated. Her educational experience had taught her that "Black people had to work twice as hard to be thought half as good." So, I had better get used to having to prove myself and be prepared to accept the challenges she knew would come. My first challenge was my sophomore English class.

* * *

A White woman with brilliant red hair and piercing blue eyes crossed the room, towered over my desk, and said, "So, you are Beverly Harris. We'll see if you are as smart as they say you are."

That statement is etched in my memory.

The first class had just started. The teacher was calling the students' names. When she got to mine, she looked around the room and hesitated, until I identified myself. Her belligerent tone shocked and embarrassed me, but I said nothing. *What was there to say?* My classmates were also silent. She stood over me for what seemed like forever, before moving away, and continuing the roll call.

That was the first day of my semester from hell. Every paper I wrote in those first weeks was returned with a "D" or "F" grade written boldly on the front but had neither comments nor corrections. Nothing indicated the reasons for the grade. After receiving the first paper, I went to the teacher.

I asked, "Could you please tell me what I did wrong to get this grade?"

Her response, "If you don't know, I can't help you."

I was stymied but did not give up. After the second paper with the same bad grade, I went back. This time her response was, "If you are so smart, you should be able to figure it out."

I was devastated because I was manic about getting good grades. I knew neither what I was doing wrong nor how to improve. Sympathetic and puzzled, my classmates asked, "Why does she hate you?" I had no idea.

Unable to resolve this alone, I went to my mother, with frustrated tears, expecting her to intervene. But, instead, she taught me a painful, but useful lesson when she said, "You will have to work this out. This will not be the only time that you will encounter someone who does not recognize your ability and potential. She is trying to break your spirit. Keep doing your work. It is fine. That is why there are no comments or corrections. You have earned a good grade, and you are going to get it. If you don't get the 'A' you deserve, then we will go to the principal. You must keep careful records of all your papers and your attempts to talk to her about them! Remember, she has something you want—that 'A'! And *you* are going to make her give it to you."

At that time, I thought my mother was cruel and heartless, but that made me even more determined to get through this nightmare. I kept detailed records. But I also kept submitting assignments and doing my best, and slowly the grades got better but still with no comments or marks on the pages. As the end of the semester approached, we received the most comprehensive assignment: a fifteen-page, type-written term paper on a subject of our choice, including an annotated bibliography, and a poem on the same topic.

This was a challenge. Therefore, I was determined that this paper represent my best work. I carefully chose a topic that I knew my teacher would consider in the mainstream of Western Civilization: "British Treatment of the Mentally Ill." I researched the topic thoroughly, read relevant sources, assembled the bibliography, took notes, and even found a poem, Rudyard Kipling's "My Mother's Son." When I handed that project in, I was proud of my work and convinced that I had exceeded my teacher's expectations.

I was right. When the project was returned, I saw the "A" grade and two words, "Excellent job!" But still no other comments. That semester ended, and I got my "A."

I had many questions: Why this sudden change? Is there any explanation for this teacher's actions other than racism or racial prejudice? Was my work markedly different than before? Did my teacher realize that she would have been unable to justify the earlier poor grades I had received if I challenged a low grade? Did she assume that I had kept records of our interactions? I will never know. But I had learned a hard lesson: Do not give up and don't allow others to define you. Looking back, I wonder how many other Black students have had similar experiences because of teachers like her? Also, how many of them had parents who could support them and be their advocates?

DISCUSSION QUESTIONS

1. How do you explain this teacher's behavior? What do you think was her intent? Does it really matter what her intent was, as the result for the student is the same?

2. What is your reaction to the narrator's mother? Do you agree with her response? Why or why not?

3. How do you imagine the narrator felt? What do you think of her behavior after the conversation with her mother?

4. What is your reaction to the conclusion? Is this the outcome that you expected? Why or why not?

5. Do you think anything should have been done about the teacher's actions? If so, what? If not, why not?

ADVISING

During undergraduate school, I confronted an unexpected situation. A junior, majoring in German Studies, I had established an impressive academic record in the department. I went to my advisor, seeking his assistance in deciding where to apply for further study. My professors had encouraged me to consider the best Ph.D. programs. The only institutions I was familiar with were the Big Ten state institutions, because I was attending one, but the Ivy Leagues were being suggested by others. So, I broached the topic with the person who I thought was best positioned to help.

At the end of my next advising session, I asked, "Prof. A., where do you think I should apply for graduate study?"

He answered, "I would strongly recommend some schools in the Big Ten because Ohio, Minnesota, and Wisconsin have excellent German Departments."

"But several professors are suggesting that I should also add Harvard, Princeton, Yale, and Stanford, since my grades are excellent, and I will have a year of study abroad under my belt. What do you think about that idea?"

He hesitated before responding, "Well, I am not sure that you are ready for that level of competition."

Surprised, I asked a follow-up, "Why not? What else do I need to be competitive?"

He paused again, "Well, you are a very good student, but I just don't know, if that's not reaching a bit too high."

I listened, thinking and wondering exactly what to make of his response. *Why was that reaching too high? He had not given me any specific reasons for his reluctance to pursue admission at these institutions. What was the obstacle that he was unwilling to name? Was it race?*

I sent those applications anyway. *What did I have to lose?* When I received both an acceptance and an offer of a multi-year Ph.D., scholarship from Stanford. I smiled, glad that I had not accepted his limitations as my own.

DISCUSSION QUESTIONS:

1. How do you explain the advisor's response to the narrator's desire to apply to Ivy League schools?

2. Should the advisor have attempted to explain his reasons to the narrator? Why or why not?

3. Do you think the narrator should have informed the advisor after receiving admission and funding from Stanford? Why or why not?

DAY ONE: TEACHING GERMAN AT STANFORD

It is the end of September 1971. My first year of graduate study ended in the spring. Working like a maniac, writing every paper and making every oral presentation in German, although not required to do so, I want to prove to everyone that I am not "an affirmative action admission." No, I have the intelligence and the German proficiency to compete with the best of my classmates. Being the sole Black student is nothing new. That was also true as an undergraduate. After a summer position at a Regional Bank in Frankfurt, my German proficiency is near-native.

Today, I am going into the classroom, the experience that I have been preparing and waiting for. After completing the Methods course, reading and rereading the Introductory German textbook, and preparing a detailed lesson plan to account for every instructional minute, I am ready. What should I wear to embody the correct balance of professional and casual? That is a complicated calculus given limited cloth- ing options and an even more limited budget. Finally, I decide upon starched jeans, a dress shirt, silk scarf, and a navy blazer. My only concession to personal style is an arm full of silver bangles.

As a young Black instructor, I know that it is critical for me to establish my authority in the classroom. I must demand respect, but this will not be easy. I am 22, only a couple of years older than my students, and I look even younger. In addition, I know that in the year 1971 most of these Caucasian students have never had a Black teacher and their only experience with Black people is interacting with them in service roles. To address this issue, I decide to employ German linguistic conventions: in my classroom, I will be Frau Harris, and address my students similarly with titles, their last names, and by using the formal pronoun "Sie," a culturally appropriate means to establish the clear boundary between teacher and students, as it is never used with family and friends.

As I walk toward my classroom, I feel a mixture of excitement and trepidation. There are lots of issues beyond my control: *Will the students accept me as their teacher? Will they cooperate with my instructional strategies? Will sudden nervousness prohibit me from completing my lesson plan?* By the time I reach the door, I conquer my fear, convincing myself that I can do this. I walk in.

Guten Morgen! (Good Morning!) *Ich heisse Frau Harris.* (My name is Ms. Harris.) Then, I write my name on the blackboard. Walking around the room, greeting each student individually with a smile, I extend my hand to shake theirs. The students are stunned by this explosion of unfamiliar sounds, since they are not sure exactly what I am saying, but slowly they begin to smile and extend their hands. We are communicating using strange words and nonverbal gestures. The class proceeds as planned, a mix of teacher modeling and student repetition, as stipulated by the prevailing foreign-language pedagogy. I finish my entire lesson plan, all in German, as required by my supervisor, and am feeling accomplished and confident.

Then the bomb drops.

In the last five minutes, I switch to English to make sure that the most important information has been understood and ask if anyone has a question. Looking around the room, I notice a rather sullen and scruffy-looking young man. Blond with shoulder-length hair and wearing the "Stanford uniform" of tattered jeans, a tee shirt, and no shoes, he is sitting near the middle of the room. Until this point, he has been more an observer of, than a participant in, the classroom activities. Now, he looks quizzical, but a bit more alert, and although he doesn't raise his hand, his body language, leaning forward with inclined head, suggests that he has a question.

So, I ask, "Do you have a question?"

"Yes," he says clearly. Then, in an impertinent tone, he asks, "When is the last time that *you* were in Germany?" (With heavy emphasis on the personal pronoun.)

A silence falls over the room, and as my grandmother often said, "you could hear a rat piss on cotton." Other students, who are already closing their notebooks, and collecting their things for a quick departure, stop shuffling and are suddenly alert. All eyes are focused on the two of us. They seem riveted by the question to which they are listening intently for an answer.

I take a long, deep breath and walk slowly from the front of the classroom to that student's chair, bend over, to look him in the eyes, and say in a loud stage whisper, "Three weeks ago, sweetie. Is that recent enough for you?"

He blushes, looking down. He responded, "I didn't mean it that way."

"I think you did, but now you know."

The rest of the class breathes a deep sigh of relief, and so do I. We have crossed the Rubicon.

DISCUSSION QUESTIONS:

1. Do you think the narrator should have been so worried about her appearance in that first meeting? Why or why not?

2. Do you agree with the narrator's assessment of her White students? Why or why not?

3. What do you make of the student's question?

4. What do you think other White students are thinking/feeling during this exchange?

5. Did you find the instructor's response appropriate? Why or why not?

6. How do you explain the meaning of the final sentence, "We had crossed the Rubicon?"

A PUBLISHER'S REP COMES TO CALL

It is my first day as a faculty member at the University of Pittsburgh. The German Department is housed in rental space, and our offices are small windowless cells. When I arrive, I see the sign on the door: "Professor Harris." This pleasant surprise fills me with pride. My first task is to make my office more welcoming and comfortable. After several months of nonuse, everything is covered with layers of dust. The bookshelves, the chairs, and my desk all desperately need my attention.

Standing on a chair, dressed in jeans and a tee shirt, a dust rag in my hand, I am attacking the bookshelves when a male voice interrupts my work with a friendly greeting.

"Hello," he says.

Without turning around or interrupting my dusting frenzy, I answer, "Hello."

The voice continues, "Is Professor Harris in today?"

"Yes."

The voice continues with another question, "When will he be back?"

"He will never be back."

The voice is silent, before it regroups, and laughing a bit nervously says, "Oh, I see. Then when will *she* be in?"

"She's in now."

The voice is silent again, for what seems a long time, before asking timidly, "Excuse me, but are you Professor Harris?"

"All day long!"

At that point, the voice says, "Uh, I will be right back; I left some books in my car."

However, he never returns.

DISCUSSION QUESTIONS:

1. What assumptions does the publisher's representative make?

2. Why do you think the narrator does not turn around to face the visitor? What might this choice suggest?

3. What is your reaction to the narrator's behavior here? Should it have been different? If so, why and how?

4. Why does the rep not return? How do you think he feels?

A MUTE MOTHER

As an assistant dean, I am always entrusted with the duties and tasks that the dean chooses to delegate. Primary among them is counseling students with academic problems and speaking with their parents. This is emotional grunt work.

One day, a mother comes to our office and approaches the receptionist with a piece of paper, on which she has written, "I speak with a dean about my son." When she is asked to provide more information about her son, she does so in writing. Apparently, she can hear, but she cannot speak. Finally, it is determined that her son has been suspended, and she wants to speak with someone about his case. Her goal is for him to return to school. The receptionist came to find me.

She apprises me of the situation as we walk from my office. But when the mother sees me approaching her, she immediately rises from her chair, backs away from me, and starts to write frantically on a piece of paper. I stop and watch her, trying to figure out what is going on. When she finishes writing, she runs over to the receptionist and hands her the slip of paper. The receptionist reads it quickly, and begins to blush a deep red. She balls up the paper and is about to discard it. However, I intervene.

"Andrea, please give me that piece of paper."

Andrea clutches the paper tightly.

"Andrea, I would like to see that piece of paper." *Why doesn't she want me to see it? What has the woman written?*

She hesitates a few moments longer, but ultimately hands it to me.

I read the almost illegible handwriting, which says "*No colored woman help me, only white woman.*"

I can feel myself getting warmer.

Unfortunately, she is out of luck. I am the only female dean in the office. Her request is insulting, but it is also ridiculous. This woman is unable to speak, yet she would rather forgo the help that she needs, than to have it come from me. How sad is that?

I then walked over to our office manager. "There is a lady here who needs to see a dean, but she refuses to allow a Black woman to help her. Would you please speak to her?"

Now, it is the office manager's turn to blush. "I will speak to her."

Our office manager approaches the woman and says, "Dean Harris-Schenz is the only person who can help you. If you do not want her assistance, I am afraid that you will have to leave." The woman looks conflicted, but then turns and leaves the office.

I wonder what happened to her son.

DISCUSSION QUESTIONS:

1. What do you imagine Andrea is feeling as she reads the note? Why does she not want to share it?

2. Should the assistant dean have demanded to see it? Why or why not?

3. How would you have felt (if you were the assistant dean) after reading this note?

4. Do you agree with the office manager's handling of this situation? Should she have acted differently? If so, how?

5. Should someone else have attempted to help this woman? Why or why not? What would "help" have looked like?

6. Should the issues of the son have been considered? If so, how?

SPEAKING GERMAN?

German is considered a difficult language to learn and speak well. After years of demanding work, I am a near-native speaker of the language. So, I delight in the astonishment of both native and non-native speakers when they hear me speak. Apparently, they find it hard to believe that an African American can master this "difficult" language.

However, it is perplexing and almost incomprehensible to experience the ways in which our mental assumptions and expectations can affect our perception. I realized that when I participated in the following three-way conversation.

One day in Germany, while looking for an unfamiliar street, I seek the help of a couple working in their yard. I walk up to them and ask in perfect German spoken at a fairly fast pace, "Excuse me, I am not from this area. Could you tell me where I could find Maximillian Street?"

The woman responds first, "I am so sorry, but I am terrible with directions, but I am sure my husband can help you. Hans, please help this young lady."

Then, Hans looks, no, stares, at me for a long time. He seems to be searching for an answer. *Why is he taking so long? This is his neighborhood, and he knows the streets.*

Finally, he responds very slowly in fractured, heavily accented English.

"If. . . you. . . speak. . . English. . . slowly, I can. . . understand. . . you."

I am confused and don't respond, because I spoke to him in his native German, not in English.

His wife, seems equally perplexed and aggravated, when she says in a loud voice, "She is speaking to you in German, not English."

Now, it is Hans who is confused. He looks first at me and then at her. Then, he asks his wife with disbelieving intonation, "She is speaking German?"

She nods, saying nothing, and glaring at him.

Then, I tried again, repeating my question to Hans. This time, after another brief pause, I get the directions that I am seeking. I thank them and walk on. Still baffled by what I have just experienced, I continue on my way.

DISCUSSION QUESTIONS:

1. Why is Hans unable to understand the narrator initially? How do you explain this?

2. How do you explain that while he did not understand, his wife did?

3. Have you ever experienced this kind of complete disconnect? If so, to what did you attribute it? How did you feel? What did you do?

ELEVATOR REVELATIONS

My office is located on the fourteenth floor of the Cathedral of Learning, and I never take the stairs. During peak class times, the elevator ride often seems interminable. But on this day, I don't mind, because the ride turns out to be quite enlightening.

I boarded the elevator on the ground floor with about 20 others, including my colleague Professor P. We are squeezed in tightly. She is a well-regarded linguist with an international reputation in social linguistics. We don't know each other well but have served on several committees and are interested in each other's academic areas. So, after a mutual greeting, I inquire, "What are you teaching this term?"

She replies enthusiastically, "A new course on Black English."

"Really? That sounds interesting."

She responds, "It is, and I have a pretty large group, including many Black students, who are invaluable as native speakers."

"Maybe, I should stop by some time." Intrigued because I had never had an academic course related to my culture.

She says, "You are welcome, but, of course, you are NOT a native speaker."

"I'm not?" *How weird, what makes her think that?*

At that point, other conversations in the elevator seem to die down and fellow passengers appear to be listening to our conversation.

She answers, "No, you were brought up in Germany on a military base."

"I was?" *Where did you get that information*? I wonder silently.

To which she responds amused, but still in a definitive tone, as if I were joking, "Yes, you know your father was an army officer and you grew up in Frankfurt."

"He was?. . . I did?" *This is getting more and more surreal.*

Our conversation has become a verbal tennis match, with spectators watching the word volley, looking quickly from one speaker to the other.

Professor P. suddenly becomes quiet and thoughtful. After a brief silence, she asks softly and rather meekly, "But, you did grow up in Germany, didn't you?"

By this time, the elevator has reached my floor, and as I exit, I respond firmly, "No, I grew up in inner-city Detroit, and my father worked at Chrysler for 30 years on the assembly line."

As the doors close, my gaze falls on the face of my colleague, Professor P. She looks both stunned and confused, but she says nothing. Neither do I.

DISCUSSION QUESTIONS:

1. How do you explain Professor P.'s assumptions about the narrator's family background?

2. What is your reaction to the narrator's thoughts and responses?

3. How do you think Professor P. feels and/or what is she thinking as the elevator door closes?

4. What are the other people in the elevator thinking about this conversation?

5. Should something happen following this conversation? If so, what and why?

"GREEKING"

For five years, I have served as the first African American female assistant dean in the College of Arts and Sciences. I consider myself an integral part of the five-person dean-team, and my four male colleagues seem to respect me and my work. Therefore, I am surprised to learn that I am being excluded from a regular gathering of my colleagues. In a conversation with Jean, the administrator to the senior dean, I inadvertently learn that "all of the other deans lunch together at a Greek restaurant near campus on Wednesdays." This event is labeled "Greeking." I am stunned because I have never heard this expression before, nor am I aware of the event.

I spend some time pondering the situation.

Why have I never been invited to attend? What is the purpose of this regular meeting? What kinds of issues are being discussed? Am I missing out on something important by not being there? What can I do to change this situation? Do I have anything to lose by confronting my exclusion head-on? The other African American dean (a male) knows that I am excluded, but he has never mentioned this to me. Has he ever said anything about this situation or is he perhaps unwilling to hazard his position as "one of the boys," by trying to include me? I decide to broach the topic with my boss at our next meeting.

My boss and I have regular meetings to discuss my areas of responsibility, so that I can update him on progress or ask questions, if necessary. We have covered the agenda items, and I am preparing to leave, when I assert my question as a planned afterthought, "Irvin, what is 'Greeking?'"

Initially, he looked a bit confused because my sudden question seems to come out of nowhere. I wait, smiling patiently. Then, I add, "I think it happens on Wednesdays."

Then, slowly recognition sets in, and he says, "Oh, that's what we call Wednesday's lunch."

"Who is *we*, Irvin?"

"The deans in FAS and CAS." He answers glibly and then realizing what he has just said, he stops, shifting in his seat and looking noticeably uncomfortable.

"Irvin, I don't go 'Greeking.' What am I?"

"An assistant dean," he answers very softly.

"That's what I thought."

I stand, hesitate for a moment looking at him, and then prepare to leave.

"Thanks, that's all I wanted to know. I have to run; a student is probably waiting for me."

As I leave his office, feeling that my mission has been accomplished, I look back to see that he is still seated at his desk, a pained expression on his face.

Before the next date for 'Greeking,' Jean calls. "The dean would like to know if you would be free to join the deans for lunch on Wednesday?"

"Thank you, that would be great," I respond.

* * *

Years later, I lectured to a group of undergraduates, sharing biographical information and how it had influenced my educational and professional development. During the subsequent question and answer period, a White male student asked a profound question: "Which do you think has had the most influence on your career—being Black or being female?"

I thought for a moment before responding, because this was a question that had never occurred to me. Then, I said, "That is a great question, and I don't mean to be flippant, but I don't know the answer because I have always been both."

DISCUSSION QUESTIONS:

1. How do you explain the narrator's exclusion from "Greeking?"

2. How do you explain the behavior of the narrator's Black male colleague?

3. How do you assess the narrator's way of raising this issue with her supervisor? How else might she have raised this with him?

4. How do you think her supervisor feels following their conversation?

5. What do you think transpired before the call from Jean? How do you think the narrator feels after that call?

6. Based on your assessment of the issues of race and gender discrimination, how would you answer the student's question?

7. How do you interpret the narrator's answer?

AN EARLY-MORNING CONVERSATION

It is my husband's birthday, and we are spending a glorious September weekend with friends at an upscale B&B in Harrisonburg, Virginia. We had arrived the night before and went to bed late. I get up early the next morning, shower, and dress to be ready for breakfast. Since it is a special occasion, I take care to dress nicely. We are still enjoying summer temperatures, so I chose a champagne-colored culotte set, with beige leather sandals, and my favorite pearl necklace and earrings. I think I am looking snazzy.

We have a large, beautifully decorated room, but since I don't want to wake Micha or let him see what I am doing, I grab my presents, wrapping paper, gift bag and card, and head to the circular sitting area that we share with three other rooms. Attractively appointed with a comfortable loveseat, an easy chair, and a small table, it is the perfect place for wrapping my gifts, undisturbed. I set to work, enjoying the quiet of the early morning. I hear one of the doors open, but don't look up.

It is not next door, so I know that it is not David and Marion's room. A male voice speaks a friendly, "Good morning."

I look up, smile, and return the greeting.

The speaker, a nearly bald older White man, is barefoot, wearing well-worn shorts, and an oversized tee shirt. He looks through the wide circular windows facing the gardens below, then turns toward me and says, "Beautiful weather today, isn't it?"

I smile again and nod in agreement. Then he adds, "We need more towels, please."

I hear his concern, but don't respond. *That isn't an issue that I can resolve.*

He waits, apparently wanting me to say something. When I don't, he re-phrases his request, as a question, "Would you bring us more towels, please?"

Then, I do answer, "Sorry, I cannot help you. I am also a guest. Perhaps, you should go downstairs and find a staff member."

He stares, hesitates a moment, says nothing, and then quickly disappears into his room.

I hesitate a moment too, wondering, why did he assume that I was an employee of this B&B?

When I finish my tasks, I go back into our room. Micha is now up and in the shower. While he dresses, I recount my morning interaction with our neighbor. He is not really surprised, but a bit chagrined. He says, "Sh-- happens, but we are not going to allow that to spoil our day." He then gives me a hug and continues to dress.

Then, our friends David and Marion knocked. When I open the door, I ask, "Do you need more towels?"

They look puzzled, and I explain that the guest across the hall has just asked me this question. David wonders, "Are you serious?"

"Yes, very," I respond.

Our friends, who are Caucasian, are a bit embarrassed and distressed. Marion says, "I am really sorry. I chose this B&B because it gets rave reviews."

"This isn't your fault. It can happen anywhere. Let's go down and get some breakfast." I don't want them to feel responsible. Today is a happy occasion, and I am not about to let the earlier episode ruin it.

We walk down the grand staircase and through the elegant hallway to the breakfast room on the first floor. I am the first in line, carrying my gift bag. I open the door to the dining room, and suddenly a hush falls on the table closest to the door. A group of people are sitting there, including my early morning interlocutor. Given the sudden silence and the strange looks on their faces, he has probably been talking about me and describing the faux pas he has committed. Forcing them to speak, I greet that table with a hearty, "Good morning. Lovely day, isn't it?"

They all look a bit pained and respond with constrained cordiality.

DISCUSSION QUESTIONS:

1. What has the male guest assumed and why? Given the scene described, do you think his assumption is reasonable? Why or why not?

2. What do you think of the narrator's response?

3. What do you think of the responses of her husband and her friends to this situation?

4. Why do you think the White guests stop speaking when the door opens?

5. What are they now thinking/feeling? What gives you this impression?

ROOMMATE

After a full year of detailed and often frustrating preparation, the adventure of a lifetime is about to begin. I had accepted the challenge and considerable responsibility of serving as an academic dean of the fall 2005 semester at Sea voyage. In over thirty years of the program, I would be the first African American female to occupy this position.

As we sailed away from Florida toward Nassau, where the 683 students would board, we were in the midst of a severe rainstorm, but we had no idea of the havoc that Hurricane Katrina would ultimately inflict upon New Orleans. The days in route to Nassau were one continuous meeting for me: faculty and staff orientation, meetings with the administrative team, introduction to the crew, and innumerable discussions to resolve the unexpected problems that demanded attention before departure. In addition, due to the worsening weather conditions, news of delayed faculty arrivals and lost baggage multiplied.

When we finally arrived in Nassau, I was convinced that the worst was behind me because our time there could be counted in hours. In the middle of students checking into their cabins and preparing to say tearful goodbyes to their families, I never expected to encounter blatant racism. But I was wrong.

As I sat at my desk completing my welcome speech to the shipboard community, a resolute knock on my door interrupted my concentration. My first impulse was to ignore it because I was almost finished. However, I didn't.

"Yes, please come in," I said, as I turned my notebook over.

Lisa, the resident director, stuck her head in, asking, "Dean Beverly, may I speak with you for a moment?"

"Sure, what's up?" I asked and smiled, trying to hide my annoyance at this interruption.

As she walked in, I could see the emergence of a solemn expression and a rather troubled look in her eyes. "I am sorry to bother you, but we have a problem. I have a mother and daughter sitting in my office, and I think you should speak with them."

Recognizing the serious tone and the concern shown on her face, I changed my tone and demeanor. "Please sit down, Lisa, and tell me what's going on."

Lisa sank into a chair and began to explain, "The student is a Caucasian female from Southern Methodist University and seems to be from a well-to-do family." *What else is new?* I thought to myself. *That sounds like most of our students.* She continued, "She has never had any experience with African Americans and has just learned that her roommate for this voyage is Black. So, she has requested a roommate change."

I took that information in. It's not that I had expected to leave racism behind me as we set out to sea, but I also hadn't anticipated it to make a grand entrance so early in the voyage.

"How do you usually handle such cases, Lisa?" I asked, knowing that Lisa was an experienced resident director and had likely dealt with similar situations before.

"Well, I explained to the mother and daughter that roommate assignments are made by matching personality profiles and common interests, and not based on race. Therefore, reassignment would not be possible."

"What was the reaction of the daughter?"

"She self-destructed! First, breaking into tears and sobbing, saying that this is totally unfair. Then, getting angry, saying that she is paying $18,000 for this semester, and she should not have to accept a roommate she doesn't want."

"What did the mother say?"

"To my surprise, she didn't say anything. She watched her daughter emote in total silence."

"What are you recommending as next steps?"

"I would like them to meet with you, and I think that will solve the problem. She certainly doesn't expect the academic dean to be a Black person. I am not going to permit a change in roommate, so she must see you, if she wishes to appeal my decision."

"Fine, I will see them." Following that rational rejoinder, Lisa got up and left my office.

After her departure, I sat for a few minutes reviewing the situation: A young White woman has signed on for a trip around the world but is unwilling to have a Black roommate. Furthermore, she assumes that this request will be readily honored and accepted as reasonable. Was that not the definition of White privilege? I sat there grappling with this situation for a few minutes. Then came another knock on my door.

I said, "Please come in," and walked around to the front of my desk to greet my visitors. Lisa was accompanied by two tanned and attractive blondes with pale blue eyes, who looked like carbon copies of each other, except one was clearly older. She presented them. "Dean Beverly, let me introduce Lindsay and her mother Mrs. R."

Well-coiffed (the elder with a sleek shortcut and the younger with thick shoulder-length hair) and tastefully dressed in what I would call casual elegance that included gold earrings, name-brand handbags, and stylish leather sandals, they greeted me. The younger woman's tentative smile and widened eyes revealed her apparent surprise at seeing me. However, the older woman looked directly at me smiling, while stretching out her hand to meet my extended one.

"Hello, I am Dean Harris-Schenz, happy to meet you both. Please have a seat," I said, as I motioned to the three chairs arranged around my desk. Since the office was not large, I returned to my seat behind the desk to subtly establish my position of authority.

"What can I do for you?" I said looking toward the student.

There was a silence, as the younger woman fidgeted in her chair, looking down and seeming a bit uncomfortable by my gaze and question.

Lisa broke the silence, "Lindsay has requested a roommate change. I denied her request, but I informed her that she could appeal my decision to the academic dean. That is why we are here."

Following that introduction, I turned my attention again, both physically and visually, to Lindsay. "So, Lindsay, why are you requesting a roommate change? Would you like to explain your reasons?" I tried to sound friendly and nonthreatening.

Lindsay answered, "My roommate is Black." She stopped, as if that was an adequate response.

"And?" I asked and waited.

"Well," she started and interrupted herself to take a deep breath, "everybody knows that Black people stink." She made this statement without any consideration that she was saying this to a Black person.

Now it was my turn to hesitate. I grounded myself by visually taking in my surroundings and focused on remaining calm and responding evenly and without emotion.

"And how do you know this? Have you met your roommate?

"No!" she answered quickly and resolutely.

"Then what is the basis for this assumption?"

"Well, I mean. . . like. . . people have like. . . told me that, who do know Black people."

"And what else have they told you?" I inquired, as softly and kindly as I could muster.

"That they steal and. . .," she continued to recount a long list of stereotypes.

When she finished, I asked, "Do you always believe what you are told, when you have no personal experience to back it up?"

"Well, no, but. . . I just don't want to live with a Black person," she responded in a manner not unlike a pouting toddler.

Changing the subject, I interjected another question. "Lindsay, why did you decide to apply to the Semester at Sea program?"

Her answer was quick and animated, "Because I wanted to see the world, experience new things, and learn about foreign countries, cultures, and their people." This response sounded almost like a TV ad for the program.

"I see." I paused and looked directly at her before continuing. "If it is your goal to learn about different people and cultures, you now have the perfect opportunity to do that right here on the ship, by having a Black roommate. This will allow you to learn about her and her culture, both of which are unknown to you."

Lindsay's eyes suddenly widened in panic, "I don't want to learn about her. I am paying all this money to travel to foreign countries. I should be able to have the roommate I want."

"No, Lindsay, if you truly want to learn about others, people different than yourself, that process will start today. I will not allow you to change your roommate. To be honest, the reasons you have given are well-known and widely perpetuated racial stereotypes, and do not at all reflect your lived experience. Now, you have the opportunity to step outside of your comfort zone and not be limited by the prejudices of others. Either you will keep your current roommate and begin this unique learning experience with us, or you will disembark and return home with your mother. You have four hours to make a decision."

Then, I turned to Lindsay's mother. "Mrs. R., would you like to say anything?"

"No, Dean, I have nothing to add. I told Lindsay that it was her decision to apply to SAS, so she has to decide whether she will go on the voyage or not."

Turning again to Lindsay, I ended the meeting by saying, "Lindsay, I sincerely hope that you will decide to remain a part of this shipboard community and join this voyage of exploration."

Then I stood up to indicate that our meeting had come to an end. I shook Mrs. R.'s hand, as she and the others left my office.

When I was alone again, I sank down into one of the empty chairs and pinched myself to see if this was reality or a nightmare. At the age of fifty-seven, I had just survived the most in-my-face example of racial prejudice of my life, and that on the first day of a 100-day voyage around the world, no less. What would the next 99 days bring?

* * *

Lindsay decided to remain on the ship.

DISCUSSION QUESTIONS:

1. Describe the narrator's feelings after Lisa presents the problem they are facing.

2. Do you think the Dean's conversation with Lisa was appropriate? Why or why not?

3. Do you agree that Lindsay's expectation that she should be able to get a roommate change is an example of "White privilege?" Why or why not?

4. What is your reaction to the Dean's behavior and language in the conversation with Lindsay? Should she have done something differently? If so, what?

5. Based on her behavior and her words, describe Lindsay.

6. What is your reaction to Lindsay's mother's behavior and words in her meeting with Lisa and the dean. Could or should she have acted differently? If so, how?

7. What is your assessment of the dean's overall handling of this situation? Might she have done something differently? If so, what and why?

8. What do you think Lindsay and her mother discussed after the meeting with the dean?

9. Why do you think Lindsay decides to remain on the ship?

NEARING DESTINATION

My husband and I travel a lot. On a recent flight to California, we reserved adjacent aisle seats, so that each of us could have more legroom and get in and out more easily. It is getting late, and we are both tired, but we have only two hours before arrival. I am fortunate because there is no one sitting in my middle seat. The nearest passenger is an older White woman, sitting at the window. When I sit down, she greets me with a smile, and we both wait to see if that middle seat will be occupied. When everyone has boarded, we share a sigh of relief that the middle seat remains empty. Micha, across the aisle, is not so fortunate. He has two neighbors. He is happy to give me his carry-on, so that it can be stored under my middle seat, giving him more legroom.

For the duration of the flight, there is continual requesting and passing of items across the aisle: mixed nuts, Kleenex, cough drops, books, newspaper and magazines, crossword puzzles, as well as tablets. In addition, there are constant conversational tidbits about this or that in German. As we approach our destination, all items are handed back and stored in the carry-on. We are about to land. The flight attendants have made the final pass through, the captain has announced that we will be on the ground in just 15 minutes. We are almost there. I sit back and close my eyes, eager to be on the ground again.

My neighbor and I have not spoken at all, other than the initial greeting, but suddenly she speaks.

In a clear Southern drawl she asks, "He (pointing at Micha) is so dependent on you, and you are so attentive to him, are *you* his caregiver?"

That is a question for which I am not prepared. We are just doing what we always do when we are together: chatting, laughing, sharing stuff. I have never considered how that might look to someone else. So, I pause to consider her observation and the related question. I take a long slow breath, smile, looking directly at the woman, and say, "I guess you could say that, since I have been married to him for 41 years."

She pales and then begins to flush dark crimson from the neck up. I continued to smile and look at her. At first, she doesn't say anything. She seems surprised by the information she has received and is struggling to process it. Or is she just trying to figure out how to respond? After a while, clearly pained, she says slowly, "Oh, I am so sorry. I didn't mean any harm."

I respond, "None was taken." I am not insulted, just surprised by her comment.

She hesitates again, seeming to search for words. "You see, I am a caregiver and have been for years."

I nod but say nothing. I don't have anything to add to her response. At that point, I lean over to Micha and say in

German, "You will not believe what just happened. I will tell you at Baggage Claim." Then, I chuckle to myself about this new situation. While this woman seemed to be giving me a compliment by praising my attention to detail and the good care that I am providing to "my patient," she has obviously totally mistaken my actual relationship to Micha. Why is that?

DISCUSSION QUESTIONS:

1. What information has the passenger acquired by watching the interaction of this couple, and what has the passenger inferred or assumed?

2. What other conclusions could she have drawn about the relationship between this male and female? What do you imagine led her to this particular conclusion?

3. What do you think of the narrator's response? How would you have responded in this situation?

4. How is the passenger feeling? How do you explain her response?

ROUTINE TRAFFIC STOP IN JUNE 2017

The street is dark, and there are few cars, though it is only 6:30 p.m. After a long day with my mother, I am returning to my hotel, already envisioning a relaxing glass of wine. I am driving on a wide, multi-lane boulevard, separated by a grassy median and bordered on each side by tall palm trees.

Although the drive is a bit longer, I prefer the peaceful surface roads to the freeway, where the long lines of traffic and aggressive after-work drivers, desperate to get home, make the commute stressful. I only have a few blocks to go. I turn on my blinker and merge into the left-hand turn lane, waiting for the stop light to change. The light turns green. As I turn into the right lane, I see the police car. He puts on his "bubble-gum machine," and I pull over, stopping to let him pass. But he doesn't pass. He pulls up behind me, saying on his loudspeaker: "Driver, pull onto the shoulder." I pull onto the shoulder and stop. He then stops his car and gets out. He walks toward my car.

Why am I being stopped? I wasn't speeding. I had used a turn signal. I have done nothing wrong! What does he want? My heart is racing, my hands tighten their grip on the steering wheel. I can hear voices telling me, "Keep calm. Speak only when spoken to. Be polite and respectful. Make no sudden moves. Acknowledge his authority. Don't escalate the situation." I am determined to sound and appear calm.

He comes and stands at the passenger window, but he doesn't speak. Taking a deep breath, I roll down the window, and ask politely, "May I help you, Officer?"

A young White man, about 30, is looking down at me.

He answers, "Ma'am, do you know that you don't have any lights on?"

"No, Officer, I thought I had lights on."

"Well, you do, but only the parking lights."

"Oh, this is a rental car. Maybe I pushed the wrong button."

"Where are you from?"

"Pennsylvania."

"May I see your driver's license?"

"Yes, but it is in my purse, behind me on the floor. May I get it?"

"Yes, of course."

"But there is no light in the car."

"I will shine my flashlight back there."

I hesitate, afraid to turn around to get my purse. I take another deep breath.

He beams a light into the back seat and asks, "Can you see it now?"

"Yes." I turn, quickly grab my purse, and say, "May I open my purse? The license is in my wallet."

"Yes, of course."

Slowly, I open my purse, find my wallet, take out the license, and pass it over to him.

"What brings you to California?"

"I am visiting my mother."

He returns my license and adds, "Well, have a nice time, but don't forget to put those lights on. I don't want someone to rear-end you."

"Thank you. Do you want to see the car rental agreement? It is in the glove box."

"No, no, that's not necessary. Take care." Then, he steps away and returns to his car. He gets into the car and drives away.

I close the passenger window and take a long, deep breath. My hands are shaking and dripping. I can't move, not yet. I am thanking God that nothing happened. I have just encountered a White policeman doing his job. He was professional and polite. Yet, I am sweating, shaking, almost hyperventilating. Too many other routine police stops have ended quite differently for drivers who look like me.

Stephon Clark, 2018

Philandro Castile, 2017

Terrence Crutcher, 2016

Walter Scott, 2015

Sandra Bland, 2015

DISCUSSION QUESTIONS:

1. What is your reaction to this story?

2. Describe the driver's reaction to/feelings about being stopped. Can you identify with her? Why or why not?

3. Have you ever been stopped by a police officer and had this reaction or feelings? Why or why not?

4. Describe the driver's behavior toward the police officer. Is this appropriate in your view? Why or why not?

5. Do you think this traffic stop would have been different had the driver been a 20-year- old Black female or Black male? In what way?

6. What might have happened during this traffic stop that could have led to a different outcome?

7. Why do you think the driver asked the police officer if he wanted to see the car rental agreement?

8. Describe the feelings/emotions of the driver after the officer leaves. Do you feel these are exaggerated? Why or why not?

EPILOGUE

Since the stories you have just read span more than 60 years, I have consulted my journals, photo albums, and yearbooks, and spoken with family and friends to fill in missing memories. Some details have been sharpened by reimagining the scenes, trying to recreate the specific atmosphere, and envisioning the people involved as well as the feelings that they evoked in me at the time. Focusing on one main event in each story has helped me to streamline the memories, the details, and the impact.

The chronological order from past to present in which I have arranged the stories here does not reflect the sequence in which I wrote them. "Routine Traffic Stop in June 2017," for example, was brought to paper first, while "Mr. Harris" and "Miss Mary," the two stories devoted to my parents, were among the last to be written. Looking at this disparity leads me to examine the process by which this collection came into existence.

I had never thought or intended to write about these situations. Nonetheless, their emergence in this form was surprisingly spontaneous and almost effortless. After completing a memoir of the first 25 years of my mother's life, I realized that I had enjoyed both the researching and writing of her story, so I decided to learn more about the art of personal narrative. I enrolled in my first course of creative nonfiction at a local university.

While mulling over the first writing assignment for that course, I was struck by the repeated news accounts of Black people being stopped by police, often with dire consequences. These incidents recalled a recent traffic-stop experience of my own. From the opening line to the concluding sentence, the story seemed to write itself as my memories of fear and anxiety flowed onto the page. It was as if the emotional flood gates had been thrown open.

To my surprise, my instructor and classmates responded favorably to my fledgling efforts and encouraged me to continue to write such pieces. Meanwhile, I was concurrently reading the writings of other Black authors who were exploring their experiences with racial bias and implicit racism. I realized I could contribute to a critical conversation, since I, as a Black female, had also encountered many such situations in my personal and professional life.

First, I made a list of situations and events that seemed relevant. Then, I sat down to write. Although the events I wanted to describe had occurred many years prior, I was able to reconstruct them easily and without the slightest hesitation. They may have lain dormant in my memory bank, but they were not forgotten. As I wrote, I could feel the same surprise, frustration, anger, or even hurt that these events had manifested years earlier. Why is that? At the time of these occurrences, I had thought they were unimportant and not worthy of my attention, even trivial in the scheme of things. I am not a psychologist, but it is apparent that to be able to remember and reconstruct these situations so easily and vividly, they must have been more impactful than I had thought initially. That is testament to the lasting effect of chronic discrimination and diminution.

My parents had instilled in me a life philosophy that has always guided my actions and choices. They taught me by their example that life is a deck of cards and each of us is dealt a hand. Their advice: Play the hand you are dealt and make the best of it, rather than whine and complain about what you don't have or wish you had. Consequently, from early in my life, I focused on taking absolute control of those things that I could, and when this was not possible, I moved on. I knew that I could do nothing about my race, my gender, and my parents' economic wherewithal. Therefore, I saw it as my duty to push myself to the limits of my God-given talents and abilities by exploring all options and opportunities to the fullest. This meant that in my daily interactions, I repressed the frustrations of "everyday racism" to the degree possible and focused my attention on moving toward the long-term goals that I had set for myself. Consequently, I relegated memories like the ones I have written about here to the outer reaches of my memory bank. What I have discovered by resurrecting and writing these stories has been an unexpected experience of simultaneously letting go and regaining control.

I have asked myself why I chose these vignettes, as surely this collection does not include all the microaggressions I have encountered. What these episodes share is a singular focus on one specific event that I could describe simply and convey clearly, without providing more context. Furthermore, although they derive from my experiences, they are like those many Black people encounter daily. Finally, because of their brevity, they are accessible and impactful, hopefully enabling readers to contemplate what they have read. In contrast, writing in more depth about the racial bias that I encountered in my professional career would have required extensive background information to create an appropriate context, potentially limiting interest to fellow academicians. I knew I wanted to reach a wider, more heterogeneous audience.

Initially, my goal for this project was intensely personal: to get in touch with long-buried parts of my life experience, and to see who I was then and who I have become. However, after sharing the writing with different readers, who generously offered their reactions and comments, my goal broadened. Black readers could immediately identify with the content and recount similar stories of their own, while many White readers expressed surprise and dismay that such events "were still happening." They had relegated such situations to a racially disturbing past that they felt had long been overcome. Still others felt strongly that these vignettes could be used for educational purposes, perhaps to spark conversations among interracial groups who were willing to engage in challenging and even uncomfortable discussions about race.

That idea intrigued me. Thanks to the generosity of the Facing Systemic Racism (FSR) Ministry Team at my church, I was able to test this hypothesis. In two separate sessions, with about 50 participants, I introduced and read my vignette "Routine Traffic Stop in 2017," which describes my experience and interaction with a White police officer. In the small and large group discussions that followed the reading, participants (who were racially and generationally diverse) engaged in active discussion. They shared their personal experiences with police stops and their reactions to the episode. Not surprisingly, their comments often coalesced along racial lines: Black participants shared my experience of fear and anxiety in reporting their interactions with police officers, while White participants reported never having personally experienced such feelings.

However, they were to a person both surprised and regretful that Black participants' experiences differed so significantly from their own. Black participants were gratified that the vignette documented and validated their lived experience; one woman commented, "I always watch my speed because I want to avoid an encounter with the police." Another asserted that "in traffic stops, I am always calm and overly polite. I want to come out alive." White participants felt that learning about the specific experiences of Black people made a more meaningful contribution to their understanding of "everyday racism" and its effects on individuals' lives and feelings; many participants reported feeling "sadness, grief, and shame, but not surprise" about the differences between their interactions with police and those of the Black participants. In conclusion, one White participant summed up the value of the vignettes quite succinctly, when she said that "having access to a true personal experience with racism made a more significant impact on me than the information that had previously been presented in sessions devoted to abstract data, reports, and statistics."

In two other sessions sponsored by the FSR [Facing Systemic Racism Ministry Team], I read, and we discussed "Buying Shoes" and "High School English." These stories describe situations in which I experienced racial bias or outright prejudice. Here too, the participants actively engaged in discussion of the issues, expressing their feelings and opinions about situations that were similar to or in stark contrast to their own lived experience.

During the pandemic, I participated in Zoom discussions and conversations with eighth- grade students in the Pittsburgh area. Initially, I was invited by the local Teen Screen Program to be a guest speaker and discussion leader for short films related to the Black experience in the United States. Since all instruction was virtual, teachers were able to utilize the expertise of educators who would normally have been inaccessible to them and their students.

Following engaged discussion of several films, I asked the teacher, Mr. Smith, if he and his students would be interested in participating in a pilot project to discuss stories from my recently completed collection of personal vignettes, describing my experience with "everyday racism." He agreed and over the course of the 2021-2022 academic year, I read and discussed four stories from my collection with his students. Two stories

"Buying Shoes" and "High School English" which presented situations from my life as a Black adolescent were especially well received. Although my experiences, with unconscious racial basis by a salesperson and outright prejudice of a teacher, were quite different from anything his predominantly White students had ever encountered, they identified with the disrespect and unfairness I felt more than 60 years ago. Feeling validated, some Black students shared their experience with racial bias. My stories elicited feelings of outrage and empathy in both groups. My discussion questions following the stories encouraged students to focus on specific issues of commonality and difference, in comparison to their lived experience.

Based on the feedback from these pilot sessions, I am convinced that these vignettes describing my personal experiences will continue to engender intense and meaningful conversations between people of different identities and ages about the feelings and issues related to "everyday racism." After reading these stories, I hope all readers will be challenged to learn about the ways in which our lived experiences differ, and that this will enable us to think about how these differences influence how we see and treat those who are not us. Becoming aware of a problem is the essential first step in considering how to solve it.

ACKNOWLEDGEMENTS

So many people have helped and encouraged me in my development as a writer and especially in the creation of this collection. The Madwomen in the Attic Program at Carlow University (Pittsburgh) offered my first courses in creative nonfiction writing. My instructors Nancy Kirkwood and Sheila Carter-Jones, as well as my Madwomen classmates provided thoughtful feedback and encouraged me to tell my stories. In my first class with Nancy, I wrote "Routine Traffic Stop in June 2017," which led to other vignettes. My writing coach, Jena Schwartz helped me to find and develop my voice. My friends Marion Kalbacker, Judie Compher, Susan Smith, Marilyn Webster, and Kipp Dawson have read multiple drafts, providing helpful and insightful comments. I have received invaluable editing assistance from both Margaret Havran and Ronald Winkler. Susan Smith also shared her technical expertise to resolve problems with text-formatting and other word-processing issues. Members of the Facing System Racism Committee and congregants of the East Liberty Presbyterian Church gave me the opportunity to read and discuss three stories in settings with diverse and intergenerational participants. Mr. Jason Smith, an eighth-grade social studies teacher, kindly permitted me to pilot four of my vignettes in several of his classes. I am grateful to him and his students for their willingness to step outside of their comfort zone. Finally, I am indebted to my husband Michael, my most severe critic and enthusiastic cheerleader, for encouraging and supporting me throughout this project.

ABOUT THE AUTHOR

"An African American German professor: an oxymoron?" No, that was Beverly Harris-Schenz's identity for thirty-eight years. A professor and administrator at three universities, Harris-Schenz was the first Black faculty member in the German departments of the University of Pittsburgh, University of Massachusetts, and Rice University. She was the first Black female appointed Vice Provost as well as Assistant and Associate Dean for Undergraduate Studies at the University of Pittsburgh, and Academic Dean of a Semester at Sea voyage. Notably, she was also the first Black instructor to many of her predominantly Caucasian students. Since retiring from her university positions, she has completed *Mary Martin: Black Government-Girl*, an essay on her mother's early life, and has published two stories "Routine Traffic Stop in June 2017" and "The Arch," the latter describing her first meeting with Archbishop Emeritus Desmond Tutu. Both stories have appeared in *Voices from the Attic*, an anthology published by Carlow University Press. She lives in Pittsburgh, PA with her husband.